# Poetry Inspired

## Volume I

Copyright © 2020 Stephanie J. Jackson

ISBN: 979-8-4541-2372-7

# Table of Contents

I Give Thanks with a Grateful Heart

A Special Thank You To

Dedication

My Reason, My Goal, and My Hope for Writing This Book

## *Glory to God*

## *The Man of My Dreams*

## *In Loving Memory*

## *Words Of Encouragement*

# I Give Thanks

## with a

## Grateful Heart

I thank God for helping me find my words,
the courage to write from the heart, and for allowing the light
of his love to shine through me to others.

# A special thank you to:

**My handsome husband:** for your unconditional love and support.

**My beautiful mom:** For allowing me to read and re-read (ad nauseam), poem after poem for her until I felt I got it right. For never once showing impatience and for always making time for me. For your never-ending love and support, and for being my biggest fan!

**My sweet friend Stefanie J.:** For your beautiful words of encouragement and support, your thoughtfulness, and most of all for having such a kind heart.

**The lovely Denise K. and her equally as wonderful husband Bill:** For your continuous encouragement and support, your enthusiasm in sharing my poetry with others, and most of all your friendship.

**Mary McConnell:** For being one of the first to see the potential in my poetry and getting my very first publication of "Unborn Apology" in the Mass. Citizens for Life newsletter. You've been a constant confidant and true supporter of my writing. Your friendship has been a blessing in my life.

**Teresa F.:** For freely expressing the emotional effect my poetry had on you. Your reaction made me realize my writing could touch lives and help others know they're not alone. You motivated me and for that I thank you from the bottom of my heart.

**Natalie H.:** For the confidence and encouragement you gave me each time you would publish one of my poems in The Criterion.

**Fr. Ricke:** For the confidence and encouragement you gave me each time you would allow my poems to be published in the church bulletin.

**Many friends and family:** For allowing me to share my poetry with them, their honest reaction and input, encouragement and support, and for those who inspired me with their stories.

# Dedication

**Eileen C. O'Grady**
**(My Beautiful Mom)**

To a woman whom I admire, respect, and love more than words can express. She is my confident and best friend. She's always been my greatest supporter in whichever decisions in life I'd make. She shares in my highs and comforts me in my lows. Her love for me has always been steadfast and true. I thank God for blessing me with such an amazing mom.

# My Mother, My Friend

MWAAAH!

Nashville, TN "Road Trip!"

# My Reason, My Goal, and My Hope for Writing This Book

**My Reason:**  For as long as I can remember it's been challenging for me to verbally express my thoughts and feelings, confidently and clearly. I'd feel self-conscious stuttering through a conversation, trying to find the right words.

I found that writing is a *wonderful* outlet for me to express myself freely, comfortably, and at my own pace. I had all these thoughts racing through my mind that I wanted to share with others. I wanted to write with simplicity, to have the words flow easily, and allow the reader to enjoy a smooth journey into my *feelings*, *opinions*, and *stories*.

**My Goal:**  I write about a vast variety of subjects. I want the poetry to be relatable to everyone in some way. I want the inspirations to make you feel like I am *speaking directly to you*. I don't want you to feel like you're just reading words in a book; I want you to feel that you're my primary focus and you're important to me, *because you are*.

**My Hope:**  It would be a *dream come true* if now with you and some day long after I'm gone, my poetry touches lives; to make you feel you are not alone in something you're going through, to promote healing, to make a necessary change in your life or someone else's, and to touch on all your emotions; but most of all My Hope is to cause a positive effect in each of you. If I can do that, then I've left a truly meaningful legacy behind that can continue on each time my book is read.

I hope you're ready to turn the page and allow me to take you on a personal journey through **Poetry Inspired,** which will hopefully open your mind, heart, and soul.

**Enjoy!**

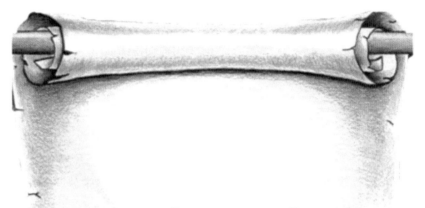

"Poetry is the music of the soul

and, above all,

of great feeling souls."

~Voltaire

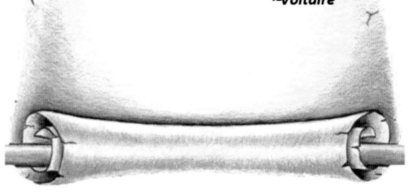

# The Words Before You

Poetry's inspired by an experience,
  thought, or a story shared.
Intended to draw out emotion
  with no one being spared.

It may cause you heartache.
  It may make you smile.
It may bring back memories
  of an earlier time, worthwhile.

You may even find yourself
  personally, relating to each word.
The writer has been successful
  if emotions are being stirred.

No matter what the effect
  when the words ring true;
try to enjoy the ride
  reading **the words before you**.

# The Words Before You Inspiration

*As a poet, I find it gratifying when my writing draws out emotion. To me the success of my poetry is determined when someone tells me they felt as if I was writing for them or about someone they know. If the reader is relating to the poem, then it becomes personal and they can't help but feel emotion.*

This particular poem was inspired by all those who took the time to share with me how my words affected them. I prefer that you'll all feel happy, comforted, motivated, or hopeful. No one wants to feel negative emotions like sadness, regret, or anger; but that's life. Feeling something, anything is good. It means you have a heart, you're reachable, and you're human; not a robot.

**Conclusion:** Of course, people inspire me, but only I know for certain whom I'm writing about unless I choose to divulge that information. I have changed names to protect others even in my self-inspired poems. No matter the person, place, or thing I write about; it is never my intention to use my words as a weapon or to cause any harm. However, if you take the *words before you* personally and don't like what you're feeling about yourself, then maybe it's time to take a long look at the person in the mirror and make a change.

# My Mother, My Friend

In the year nineteen sixty-two,
    being unwed and pregnant wasn't easy to do.
Rounding the corner into a brand-new year,
    caused mixed emotions of anxiety and fear.

You made the choice to keep me
    and raise me on your own.
My father denying me,
    you felt betrayed and alone.

You were turned away by family
    and those you called friend.
Feeling that disappointment and rejection
    was never going to end.

The day I was born,
    adoption and money were offered to you.
You held your head high,
    to me, you stayed steadfast and true.

As the years passed by,
    it was always me and you.
You gave me a good life,
    doing what you needed to do.

You worked so hard
    and continued to stay strong.
Making certain I needed for nothing,
    with you where I belonged.

We've certainly experienced
   life's highs and lows together.
Our mother, daughter bond
   continues to grow and will live on forever.

You tell me you're proud
   of the woman I've become.
And having me
   is the best thing you've ever done.

It is I, who is proud
   of the woman you are.
Not only as a mother, but as a person
   you surpass many by far.

You're a loyal friend.
   You have a good heart.
You're loving, caring, and have a sense of humor
   that is set apart.

You're thoughtful and generous,
   putting your own needs last.
When you're in pain,
   you wear a smiling mask.

Your character is strong.
   Your values are high.
You have a sensitive soul.
   You easily cry.

With those whom you love
   and who've earned your respect,
you've touched their lives
   with a positive effect.

From the moment we met
    and long after you're gone,
a special place in my heart
    is where our bond will live on.

A relationship like ours
    will never come to an end.
You're **My Mother**, my confidant,
    **My** forever **Friend**.

# My Mother, My Friend Inspiration

*This poem is very near and dear to my heart. My beautiful mom is the strongest woman I know. She went through challenges in life that would've hardened most people. She kept a tough exterior for many years, never allowing vulnerability to surface due to heartbreaking disappointments from those she trusted and loved. Even with me, the one exception in her life, complete unconditional trust took time. The barrier finally came completely down with me when she was in her seventies.* **Her seventies!**

*I'd like to share with you how she overcame to become the selfless, generous, thoughtful, kind, charitable, funny, admired, well-respected woman she is today. This same woman has <u>always</u> been a devoted, loving mother whose tough exterior would come out in full force as a fierce defender to anyone who hurt or tried to hurt me. She was a force to be reckoned with, but that's another story.*

She was always a hard-worker. As a single mother it was the norm for her to work multiple jobs. Even though we didn't have much money, she was a good provider. We had a roof over our heads, warmth in the winter, food on the table, and most importantly we had each other. I didn't have any siblings but we lived in a neighborhood with a lot of children to play with. Mom always made sure I had activities like ice skating, swimming, dance classes, and religious education; all to keep me well-rounded and happy. When I got a bit older mom took classes to get her G.E.D. in the hopes of pursuing better job opportunities. She was motivated to improve herself and our lifestyle. It worked. She ultimately moved up into a management position at a local supermarket which allowed her several perks such as; a company car, insurances, more money, bonuses, and additional education.

During my sacrament of confirmation, she met a woman (E.T.), a nun who became her best friend and changed her life again, for the better. She's also a strong, independent woman with exceptional moral values and character. They were quite the duo. Their friendship opened up a whole new world for my mom. When I was living on my own and enjoying the life of a single young woman in my 20's, mom felt free to do some living of her own. She and E.T. went on all sorts of fun trips together; she even flew for the first time in her life going to Italy with a church group. She went to Haiti and met the truly poor, yet devout people in the villages. She went to Colorado to share in the Pope's Mass during a World Youth Day celebration. In between her adventures, she became a mentor as a T.A.P (Teens Against Pregnancy) leader through a church youth group, C.O.T.Y. (Church Outreach to Youth). She was on the board of directors of C.O.T.Y. for years. She also signed a covenant and became an Associate of the Sisters of St. Joseph. She was living a new, exciting life. Her faith in God was growing and E.T. became a trusted friend. *A TRUSTED friend*! That was big. **A barrier came down.**

During the changes in both of our lives we remained connected and close. We'd often go on road trips that we liked to call mother-daughter get-a-ways. We'd have so much fun together! Mom always had a sense of humor that knew no boundaries. It was a wonderful way to take a break from our individual lives and reconnect. To this day either one of us will echo those familiar words, *"It's time for a ROAD TRIP!"*

Over the years mom changed jobs several times. Some not by choice, but most were. Nearing the end of her working life, she primarily worked in the service of the elderly and sick in nursing homes; entertaining them, making them laugh, feel less lonely, and forgetting their pain for a short time. When becoming semi-retired, she decided to work part-time for a home care company where she performed numerous duties caring for her clients. Mom would always go out of her way to make anyone she was caring for feel safe, comforted, and extra special.

At the age of seventy, mom had her first surgery. This was a huge ordeal for her because she was terrified of anything medical. She had always managed to avoid (escape) it, *but not this time.* It was literally a life-or-death decision. Her fear was getting the best of her and she was close to making the wrong choice. I told her not to worry about anything. I took over. I left my home and husband to stay with her for all the pre-op testing, the surgery, and the post-op care for a total of six weeks. *She needed me and I wasn't going to let her down.* She was brave and she/we got through this together! When it was over and she was recovered; I was getting ready to fly back home and she said to me, *"I trusted you to take care of me, to take care of every detail, and you did. I felt safe with you and I always will. I believe I recovered faster because of you. I trust you in every aspect of my life. I will never doubt you."* **Another barrier came down.** Even though we were always close and I had never given her reason not to trust me; it took her a lifetime to truly be free and allow someone else to take control, *to take care of her.*

Early on and with good reason, mom had always been suspicious of men's intentions. Due to her own experiences and male role models in her life, she came to the conclusion that they were self-serving and untrustworthy. *That was until my husband changed her way of thinking.*

He not only takes great care of me; he takes great care of her. He respects our close relationship and has always gone above and beyond to do what he can to make sure she has everything she needs. He loves her and the feeling is mutual. He accomplished the unimaginable and won her trust, **another barrier down.**

After several surgeries, multiple health issues, and much encouragement from my husband and me, mom made the decision to officially retire. This was an extremely difficult decision for a woman who has worked her entire life. It was time to let go of a sense of security for her and allow two people whom she loves and trusts to help her do so, **another barrier down.**

**Conclusion:** I am so proud of my mom. She overcame and has lived a wonderful life, opening up to new friendships, growing in her faith in God, being a caring humanitarian, and breaking down the barriers of trust. Most of all, I am proud to be her daughter. Through all of life's highs and lows, she and I have always been there for each other. I feel truly grateful to God for not only giving me such an amazing mom who selflessly took care of me as a child and who became a close confidant and friend as an adult, that He, Himself was constantly working in her life and taking care of her; *taking care of us.*

I pray that when the time comes for mom to say goodbye, she trusts God to peacefully take her home, allowing the **final barrier down.**

**I'd like to add some "Fruit for Thought."** It took my mom a lifetime to truly be free of the emotional hurt she endured by the actions of others. Please be thoughtful of your actions because you never know just how deeply it could affect someone's psyche, someone's life.

# Forgiveness

You were told the news that you would soon be a dad.

You promised you'd take care of us, you seemed even glad.

Soon after, a rumor was told to you on a fateful day.

That I wasn't yours, your ego was bruised; there was a price to pay.


You left my beloved mother unwed, confused, afraid, and lonely.

Even when she said you were her one and only.

From the woman you once loved and your unborn child, you walked away.

Leaving us alone, breaking your promise to stay.


Years later when we spoke on the phone,

Forgiveness for my mom was not in your tone.

There might've been a chance, if forgiveness was in your heart.

Without it, a father-daughter relationship could never start.


Although biological, you were never my dad.

It's true what they say, "You don't miss what you've never had."

However, you missed out on the best of us

because of lies, your ego, and lack of trust.

You passed from THIS world in 2002.

    After all that's been said and done,

Yes, Leo;

    I do **Forgive** you.

# Forgiveness Inspiration

*I remember at a very young age asking my mom why I didn't have a dad. Although I never really felt the absence of a father figure in my life, I felt confused when I was in grade school and all my friends would talk about theirs. Mom would give me brief, vague answers that somehow appeased me at the time. It wasn't until I was older that the true, much more detailed reason was shared.*

I could see the anguish in my mom's face as she told me about the man (I'll call him Tim) who lied to my father (Leo, true name) about her being unfaithful. My mom had denied Tim's advances which to Tim was a shot to his ego; after all he was a self-proclaimed *"God's gift to ALL woman," how dare she refuse him!* She always thought this was his revenge on her and without knowing for certain; I agree. It wasn't the lies of an arrogant egomaniac that hurt my mom so deeply; it was the fact that Leo believed Tim over her. Leo moved on with complete disregard for us. I will never forget the tears in my mom's eyes as she relived this difficult time in her life to give me the answers I was looking for.

She admitted that over the years Leo had realized I was his child and wanted to see me. Being young, still hurt, and fearful that he'd try to take me away from her; she denied him the opportunity. When I was an adult, she offered to reach out to his sister and try to set up a meeting for us. I agreed and soon after, Leo called me.

I remember feeling so many emotions when he called. *I mean, wow; this is my father who I was speaking with.* We spoke for a long time. He assured me that I was conceived from love.

 This was a comfort to both mom and I. It was also bittersweet to know that lies, ego, and mistrust ended something beautiful. He shared his version of the events that led to the demise of his relationship with mom, which were similar. Although he knew I was his child, he still believed mom was unfaithful and that was unforgiveable. Again, it all came full circle to the day he chose Tim's lie over mom's truth. He wanted us to meet but refused to allow my mom to come with me. That was unacceptable for me. I wasn't comfortable meeting him without her. After all these years it was evident that he still had no forgiveness in his heart for her. *It's sad.* Possibly he just didn't want to relive or face the reality of his past, my mom. I'll never know. We never met. He passed away in 2002.

** Shortly after we spoke, he sent me a card with the closing salutation, "Love Dad." *Would you consider this sweet or inappropriate?* It's something I used to often ponder. **

**Conclusion:** I tried to reach out several times over the years after we spoke, but he never responded. Yes, because of my insecurity and stubbornness I missed the opportunity to meet Leo. I didn't realize that would be my last chance; *that he would shut me out as well.* Sometimes I regret not meeting him under his terms, but I needed time to absorb all the information. I needed patience and understanding. *Something a dad would give, right?* To me, that's a big difference between biological and the real deal. I find myself feeling sorry for him. *Why?* Because I once heard someone say that *forgiveness can't change the past but if given a chance it can change the future.* Mom eventually forgave him. I forgave him. He chose not to forgive and missed out on the best of me, the best of us.

**To answer your question:** I know some of you are wondering how I can be certain that my mother is telling the truth rather than Leo's friend, Tim.

Here's how; my mom and I are close confidants. She has shared the story of her life with me; holding nothing back. With that stated, there is no reason why with everything she has shared with me that she wouldn't honestly tell me if she had cheated on Leo. She could've easily said; "Yes, Leo is your father but I did cheat on him during our relationship." Never once did she ever falter from her original story. *I believe her.*

**As for Tim:** Who cares?

## Unborn Apology

My thoughts travel back to that December day.
  I made the choice to take your life away.
You weren't allowed to build your own life's story,
  For that, little one, I am truly sorry.

I was so afraid, unsure, and young.
  For my very own life had just begun.
My choice was made in the year nineteen eighty-three.
  In June of this year, you'd be turning thirty.

Would you have been a boy?
  No, I'm sure a girl would've been my pride and joy.
I daydream of the woman you might've been then start to feel blue.
  Hearing my own mom telling me "The best thing I ever did in life was you."

I've thought about you throughout my entire life and attempt to make amends.
  I will continue to do so until my own life story ends.
If I'm blessed someday to finally meet you, and I pray that I do.
  Please find it in your heart to tell me I'm forgiven, so I can respond with; "I've always loved you."

# Unborn Apology Inspiration

*What do you think of this woman? Do you think her weak and/or selfish? Do you sympathize with her? Do you condemn her for the decision she made? Perhaps you see someone you know in her. Perhaps, even yourself. It's obvious the decision she made years ago has caused her to lament and try to redeem herself in some way. It's a decision that for most doesn't come without much thought. For some, it's tormenting because of their religious beliefs. For others, it's easy and used as a form of birth control.*

*For her it was a combination of fear, betrayal, and her personal situation. Here is her story.*

Even though his words were of love, his actions were completely opposite. Shortly after ending their relationship, she met with him at his request. She still loved him. That night she had a moment of unprotected weakness and made the mistake of trusting him to stop. It came as no surprise when the doctor gave her the news. Her heart was pounding. The adrenaline was rushing through her body. Panic was taking over. She began to hyperventilate. Her world just stopped for that moment in time. *This couldn't be happening!*

Then the questions started to flood her thoughts. How could she have been so careless? How could she let this happen? Should she keep the baby and try to raise it on her own? Did she even want to be a mother now? What were her options? How does she tell her family? Should she tell him? She hadn't even heard from him since that night.

She decided to tell him. His reaction was cavalier and condescending. *She was now his possession and his plan was successful.*
Her fate was sealed and he was feeling like the master of his conquest. She now felt more trapped and alone than ever. She was young with her whole life ahead of her. Everything was about to change and, in her mind, not for the better. To make things worse, the thought of being connected to him for the rest of her life through this child was unbearable. She needed to be free from both.

The decision was made. She never told him. She lied by telling him she had a miscarriage. Only then did he attempt to connect with her and to his dismay, without any success. She was damaged.  She was depressed and weepy for months. Years later she spoke with her priest.  After a tearful discussion and reliving the events of that difficult time in her life, she was absolved. Even though she knows she's been forgiven, the pain of her choice will live with her forever and never completely heal.

**Conclusion:**  We've been given the freedom of choice. It can be a blessing as well as a hardship.  Don't take this privilege lightly. Be thoughtful in making decisions. Take into consideration the repercussions of your actions.

# Final Goodbye

You were my first,
   but not my last.
I think of you
   when I glimpse my past.

We shared some highs
   but too many lows.
So much heartache
   and tear-filled woes.

I learned a lot
   from our time together.
What I *DIDN'T* want
   and that I deserved better.

Life for you was a constant party.
   You had an addiction.
You couldn't see it for yourself.
   Our end was an obvious prediction.

I know the blame
   isn't completely on you.
After all, a failed relationship
   usually takes two.

I saw you years later.
   We had long been estranged.
Your looks were rather worn.
   Your lifestyle hadn't changed.

We move forward with our lives.
    We learn to forgive.
Remembering the lessons of mistakes,
    we don't want to relive.

To learn that you are gone,
    caused a sympathetic sigh.
I pray you're now at peace
    as I whisper a **Final Goodbye**.

# Final Goodbye Inspiration

*What comes to mind when you think of your first love? Did you really love this person? Did you even know what love was? If you were young like me, then your answers are probably yes. At least you thought so at that time. After all, when we're teenagers, don't we know "everything"? Most people I speak with about their first love memories are enthusiastic and copious when sharing details, always with a smile. Some are still with their first and have been for a lifetime. My story is quite different.*

I was a recent high school graduate ready to enjoy my summer. He was cute and fun, but because my friend liked him, I backed off. Without any encouragement he made advances towards me, which upset my friend tremendously. So much so, that she made the *mistake* of threatening me. That's when I decided to date him and lose my friend. I never had a steady boyfriend before. This was new and exciting for me! It was fun going to parties and meeting new people. Little did I know the partying would become a way of life for him.

I spent over two years with him. The parties never stopped. The only things that changed were my feelings for him and his treatment of me. Addiction took control over his life. He became emotionally abusive. I attempted to break things off several times, but he wouldn't let go and I wasn't strong enough to walk away. I got sucked in by the tearful pleas, asking me to give him another chance. Each time I agreed, I felt trapped in a vicious cycle that worsened at each attempt to start over. In my mind the only way I could finally be free of him is if I rebounded. That's what I did. Being with someone else kept him at bay while distracting me from our history. (Refer to the poem entitled-*Abuse* and its Inspiration)

Living in a small town it's easy to know about the business of others. We had both moved on, but his lifestyle hadn't changed. Years later I returned to my hometown for a visit and saw him at a local store. It was evident that we were surprised to see each other; we exchanged niceties. He looked worn and it's quite possible he was ill then.

I was saddened by the news of his passing. Not because I felt a loss but because I felt sorry for him. I was told he was ill for a while. I don't even know if his death was related to his addiction, however; if I had to take a guess I'd say yes.

**Conclusion:** Addiction is an illness that comes in many forms. It affects everyone around you, especially those closest to you. It's unfortunate that addiction and all its demons are the memories I have of him. However, writing *Final Goodbye* gave me closure of his passing.

# Abuse

I met you on the rebound
 after a bad romance.
You were attractive and fun.
 I took a chance.

Spending time together,
 I felt I knew what you were about.
Until you reeled me in
 and your true colors came out.

You spewed confidence.
 You were charming.
But your possessiveness and temper,
 were quite alarming.

You took away my voice.
 You were quick to accuse and criticize.
You took away my freedom of choice.
 I feared someday you'd be my demise.

You told me how to dress
 and who I could speak to.
If I dared speak my mind,
 I'd soon be bearing the colors of black and blue.

You spoke of love,
   how we were meant to be.
Your actions spoke louder than words,
   as you raised your fist to strike me.

You'd leave me wondering,
   "Would this be a good day?"
Never knowing what innocent action or statement
   meant a price I'd have to pay.

I lived in constant fear wondering,
   "When was the next beating?",
or when I would learn of your other bad habit
   of continuously cheating.

You were cruel, insensitive, and carried a needy ego.
   Not surprising, you were a selfish lover.
It's true what they say,
   "You can't judge a book by its cover."

So many times, I tried to leave you.
   *Just walk away.*
You'd track me down, cry,
   and implore me to stay.

You preyed on my weaknesses and my lack of self-esteem.
   So, I'd give you another chance.
Once my defenses were down again,
   you'd begin another tormenting dance.

You left me belittled, feeling worthless,
   and often bruised.
I was a shell of a person;
   emotionally, verbally, and physically abused.

My last and best day with you,
   I kept your false entreaties at bay.
The day I became strong, never looked back,
   and finally, *just walked away.*

# Abuse Inspiration

*We all make mistakes, right? We get caught up in a whirlwind of events and then neglect to see what is right in front of us. Sometimes it's the good; sometimes it's the evil. Either way, we miss it. If it's the good, we hope we're not too late to get another chance. If it's the evil, we hope the damage done can be repaired. For me, it was the evil.*

I was rebounding; struggling to find an escape from a damaged relationship that I was too emotionally weak to walk away from. My first impression of him: he was tall, dark haired, nice dresser, handsome; a myriad of physical attributes. Although my ex was attractive in his own right, this guy left me breathless; and honestly, a bit intimidated. The rebound began. He was the perfect distraction.

He was fun and exciting. I was experiencing new things. I was going dancing, four wheeling, hiking, going to the beach, traveling, Parties (without the drama), and meeting a whole new set of people. I was being swept off my feet. He won my trust. He was no longer just a rebound.

**Then it all changed:** He became possessive and demanding, insisting I stay home when he was out and about. Our interactions with others started to dwindle and were almost nonexistent. When we did go out, he would criticize my choice of attire. He would get angry when I would speak to other men or if another man showed me any attention. Not angry with them, but with me. I was slowly losing myself, again! I was being controlled and manipulated into submission, but why? Was it me; somehow my failure? Then it happened, my worst nightmare. The verbal and emotional abuse progressed into physical. It started with slaps that turned into punches.

**My worst memory:** We were at a party at his neighbor's home. To my surprise, most of the guests were his ex-girlfriends. He was at his cruelest. At a time when I needed his reassurance the most, he flirted with them and ignored me; but all the while he would make sure I was watching, as he'd smile. I made the mistake of confronting him on his behavior in front of his harem of exes and his buddies. The price I paid was a beer bottle thrown at me in full force striking me on my chest. It literally knocked me to my knees. I am ashamed to say, I still didn't leave him. I got sucked in again. It just goes to show you just how fragile I was; many may simply say.... just how stupid I was.

**The final straw:** I had the audacity to confront him on his endless cheating. He knocked me down and I hit my head hard on the ground. As I looked up at him with slightly blurred vision, I could see him laughing at me. I remember being home rocking back and forth in my chair, crying. At that point the light FINALLY went on. I was afraid of him. I knew that if I stayed with him, I'd have a life sentence of abuse and heartache, or even quite possibly; he might be my demise. Even worse, I truly believe he'd feel no remorse. Abusing me came too easy for him.

**An empowering moment:** I refused to speak with him. I ignored all calls. I returned everything to him; including the engagement ring. (Yes, I almost married him!) His attempts to reach me seemed endless. After I felt strong enough, I took his call.

He expressed his usual tearful regrets and promises. I felt nothing this time. I let him go on and on without interruption. When he asked me if I was still there, I told him I was just listening. When he exhausted all he wanted to say and waited for me to speak; all I could ask him was "Are you done?" When he said yes, my reply was simply "So am I." Then I hung up. I felt so empowered, relieved, and free!

**Conclusion:** It's easy to look at any person who stays in an abusive relationship and wonder, "What the hell is wrong with them?" "How can he or she put up with that?" "Why don't they just leave?" It's easy to judge when you haven't been through it personally or you have but were strong enough to walk away. In my case the only logical reason I can think of is that I was emotionally submissive. However, I was pleased in finding the strength to detach myself, to leave him and that destructive relationship. Like I first wrote when I started this inspiration: *we all make mistakes, right?* Learning from them is what matters. After two dysfunctional relationships in a row; one with an addict and one who was physically abusive, I knew what I *"didn't"* want in a relationship. I learned to watch for the warning signs. I became a strong, independent woman. I got my confidence and self-esteem back. I learned that I deserved to be loved. My life, needs, and desires mattered, and my love was worthwhile for not only myself but for the right person. I would never settle again for anyone who couldn't make me happier than I could make myself. I would much rather be single and sometimes be lonely; rather than be with someone who made me miserable or was detrimental to my health.

I was fortunate to be blessed with a great support system of friends and family. It took some time but the emotional scars healed. Never forgotten, but faded into my past. Over time, I have forgiven those who've hurt me; in return I have gained peace.

After years of being guarded; God gave me an amazing gift in the abundance that can only come from Him. (Refer to poems: *A Dream Come True, An Answered Prayer,* and *One True Love*-located in the section entitled *"The Man of My Dreams."*)

**My hope:** Anyone reading this who is either going through this themselves or knows someone who is, finds some comfort in knowing you're not alone. Find help through friends, family, support groups, and/or local organizations specifically designed to assist in this matter. Make the decision to take control of your life. *You're worth it!!*

**Confucius Quote:** Our greatest glory is not in never falling, but in rising every time we fall.

# Neighbor Harley

Swinging on my porch swing,
    just barely six years old.
Feeling safe in my surroundings,
    unaware of evil to unfold.

I trusted you neighbor Harley;
    thinking you were my friend.
You had a diseased mind,
    fooling everyone while you'd pretend.

You hurt me neighbor Harley.
    Forcing together what didn't fit.
A child who didn't understand;
    the heinous crime you'd commit.

You offered me several gifts,
    bribing me not to tell;
and scaring me into believing
    I would go to hell.

Once I got to mom,
    I shared your secret sin.
Soon you went to jail
    and caged the demon within.

Overcoming this act against me,
    my future you didn't take.
Life is full of happiness
    and unaffected by your mistake.

Moving on with your life,
    did truth set you free;
or did conscience haunt you
    causing you pain and misery?

I heard you passed away.
    That wasn't sad for me.
I wonder if you're at peace
    or in torment, **Neighbor Harley**.

# Neighbor Harley Inspiration

*Picture an apartment building in a close-knit neighborhood, not poor but not quite middle class, where everyone looks out for one another. They're all involved in each other's lives through gatherings, support, and friendships. There's a single, hardworking mother living on the first floor with her six-year-old daughter. Needing to work a short afternoon shift, she entrusts her only child to the care of her upstairs neighbor to watch her for a few hours, like so many times before. No one could've predicted what happened on that fateful day. A day that forever changed their neighborhood, a day that shattered innocence.*

After her mother left for work, the little girl (I'll call her Stacy) asked her babysitter if she could play in the yard where she loved to practice her dancing. Of course, she was permitted to do so. Stacy loved to dance and was in recitals each year. Once she finished practicing, she decided to swing on her own porch swing which was located just under the porch of her upstairs babysitter. Unfortunately, the swing broke. She noticed that her next-door neighbor Harley was home. He was seventeen and someone she liked, trusted, and felt safe with. He was a friend. She went to him and asked if he would fix her swing. He invited her into his apartment while he got the tools he needed. He asked her if she'd like to see his room. Innocent and trusting, she agreed. Even though she was just a child, she began to sense things weren't right and said she'd wait for him by her swing. That's when he pushed her on to the bed and pulled down her pants. He exposed himself, spread her little legs, and attempted to enter her. She was too tiny to penetrate so he flipped her over and attempted to enter her anally. It all happened so fast for this sweet little girl. She was in shock!

At that point and much too late, Harley had a moment of conscience and stopped. The reality of what he was doing surfaced and he began to panic. In the background they could hear the babysitter calling loudly, "Stacy!" in almost a frenzied voice. Harley was trying to calm a crying Stacy with apologies and bribing her with gifts. Before allowing her to leave, he made her promise not to tell anyone. Knowing she believed in God, Harley told her that this was to be their secret and if she broke her promise; she would go to hell. She never told her babysitter.

Not until she was surrounded with the safety of her mom, did she tell her secret. Even then, she told her indirectly at first. Her mom and a friend took her to the drive-in movies that night where a double feature would often be shown. The first was usually for children, the second for adults. During the adult feature, Stacy would lay down on the back seat with a blanket and pillow and go to sleep. Not this time. She heard moans and looked up to see a man on top of a woman. Stacy said to her mom, "That looks like the man is trying to put his thing in her thing, mommy." Alarmed by this statement, her mom asked her what made her say that. That is when she told her secret.

Immediately, Stacy was brought to the emergency room where she was thoroughly examined. The physician stated that she was bruised both vaginally and anally, but no penetration had occurred. She was a very lucky little girl because if Harley was successful in his attempts, he could've caused serious injury and possibly death. He added that although she would recover physically, it is quite possible she may struggle emotionally. As time passes the incident could become dormant in her memory, but could surface when she's an adult, affecting her relationships and intimacy.

Harley was arrested. When asked why he did it he said, "I was watching Stacy dance in the yard and looking through a Playboy magazine. I got turned on." This is certainly a statement from a teenage boy who had definite emotional issues. Never-the-less, he was to pay for his crime against an innocent child and he did. His mother stood by him and defended his actions, stating it was all Stacy's fault. What?! This completely enraged Stacy's mother. The relationship between the two mothers had changed forever. The actions of Stacy's mother caused several unfortunate happenings (although deserving) in Harley's mother's life, causing her to relocate. The close-knit neighborhood was never the same.

**Conclusion:** That season in Stacy's young life was undeniably tragic, but it didn't ruin her. Stacy beat the odds against her and grew up to be a well-rounded woman. She has formed strong, healthy relationships with family and friends; and yes, she is happily married.

**Helpful Information:** When writing this poem and inspiration I found a website that I hope will be useful if you or anyone you know might suspect a child is being abused. For more information go to www.rainn.org, (Rape, Abuse, Incest National Network) or call 800-656-HOPE (4673) for 24/7 Help. Or, you can call Child Protective Services or Social Services. You may even choose to be anonymous if necessary. *Please don't hesitate.*

Pedophilia is a sexual attraction to pre-pubescent children. If you suspect someone of this, there are a lot of resources online that can assist you on taking steps to help prevent a child from being hurt. I found www.stopitnow.org, which I thought had good information. You can always call your local police or the services mentioned above. *Again, please don't hesitate.*

# Patience is a Virtue

Two days prior;
   I receive a familiar call,
to confirm my appointment;
   the usual protocol.

I arrive early,
   as I was requested.
The waiting room is full,
   I notice patience is tested.

The reason is clear
   from the sign-in sheet.
Several double bookings revealing
   a tough schedule to meet.

This is my theory,
   something to think about.
Something to consider
   before you pout or even shout.

We, their patients;
   outnumber them three to one.
They prepare for us
   even before our appointment has begun.

Some of our appointments
   are follow-ups or routine,
while others have needs more urgent
   or it's crucial to be seen.

The medical results
    that weren't benign.
The doctor answering questions
    taking the time to be kind.

Another patient being told;
    you only have 6 months to live.
The doctor and staff take the time
    to offer all the compassion they can give.

How about the gentleman
    who just lost his wife?
Stricken with such grief,
    speaking of taking his own life.

Be understanding and kind
    even when it's a chore.
The next time they run behind,
    it could be you behind that closed door.

We all have busy lives
    and places to be.
Each life is precious
    embracing its own story.

At your next doctor's appointment,
    think about the patients before you.
Be courteous, and remember
    patience is a virtue.

# Patience is a Virtue Inspiration

*I used to work in a medical office alongside hard-working individuals, all trying our best to keep up with a hectic schedule. Everyone from reception to the nurses and doctors made up a stellar team of caregivers; I know firsthand the many steps there are to prepare for each patient.*

On any given day which is almost every day, the schedule changes due to *"must see"* patients that *"in their opinion"* can't wait another day to be seen even though they've been suffering with a sore throat for a week. Then there's the truly urgent, *must-see* patients that call the doctor out of the office to the hospital; resulting in a full rearrangement of the schedule.

There will always be the patient that checks in and says, *"Is the doctor running on time? I have to be some place so I can't wait."* My all-time favorite statement is, *"My time is just as valuable as the doctors so why do I have to always wait past my scheduled appointment?"* Here's a thought; if you already know it's more likely than not you will need to wait, why not plan for it? On the *"off"* chance you are able to get in and out on time, how wonderful for you! Actually, how wonderful for all of us. That would mean no emergencies or patients in crisis.

It's frustrating to listen to individuals piss and moan about delays, especially when we who are on the other side of the waiting area, know the doctor is taking the much needed, necessary time to comfort, reassure, answer questions, and quite honestly; doing their best to be a compassionate, professional caregiver. Aren't the lives of those patients that need more time worth it? *Would you be worth it?*

**Conclusion:** Your medical team is there to take care of you. That's exactly what it is combined with you, a team effort. Be patient. Be understanding. Try planning ahead to make time to *"wait."* Instead of complaining, be joyful and pleasant because you don't know what the person sitting next to you is going through. Not everyone is there for routine care or something minor. If someone checked in after you and *IS* being difficult, try offering them the option to go ahead of you and take *your* scheduled appointment. After all, you don't mind waiting. It just might cause them to pause and rethink their behavior. Say thank you to everyone as you leave. Most of all; be grateful it's not *YOU* that's causing the delay.

# Homeless

Whether you're in a small town
   or in a big city,
You see them on street corners,
   You look upon them with pity.

Holding up their signs
   trying to tell their story;
of hunger, needing a job,
   or a veteran fallen from glory.

Some people are cruel
   speaking hurtful comments,
walking by the street homes
   made of cardboard tents.

"Don't give them money!"
   They shout as their body shrugs.
They'll only spend it all
   on alcohol and drugs.

There's a story behind
   each sad face.
Remember, we're all part
   of the same human race.

Each life is precious, fragile,
   and deserves respect.
We need to give the benefit of the doubt,
   and what's left of their dignity, protect.

It could be addiction
 that brought them to this place.
Maybe hardship, depression,
 or a devastating loss could be the case.

Before you pass judgment
 and ride off on your high horse;
stop and think
 of an alternative course.

If money is not something
 you can or want to share;
there are other ways
 to show that you care.

A friendly smile as you walk by
 and acknowledge their existence.
Volunteer at a shelter.
 Your time can make a difference.

We're all God's children,
 no matter what our circumstance.
When you see someone homeless,
 consider their story and give kindness a chance.

# Homeless Inspiration

*I was in my early twenties and in Boston, Massachusetts at a work-related convention when I saw homelessness for the first time. I had only heard about it through conversations and seeing it on television. It was heartbreaking to see it up close and affecting so many. When I was approached and asked if I could spare some change my initial instinct was to help, but those I traveled with advised me not to. They stated I would soon be surrounded by many; it would be overwhelming and risky with the likelihood of them purchasing drugs and/or alcohol rather than food, clothing, or even shelter for an evening. Young and in unfamiliar territory, I conceded.*

*The experience continued to resonate making me realize that each of those sad faces had a story. The lack of compassion I witnessed was disturbing. No one wants to be without shelter, food, water, and clean clothes; our basic human needs. Then to add insult upon injury be treated with cruelty, verbal abuse, and in some cases physical abuse.*

I began to fabricate my own stories for how they came to this place in their lives:

There's a middle-aged woman sleeping in a car full of personal items because the local shelter is on a first come first serve basis and is always full during the unforgiving New England winters. She's grateful to have her car and a place to lay her head at night to feel some sense of safety. I see the scars and bruises on her face. She's been abused and battered for years, but this life is better than the one she left behind. *Have you ever seen this woman before?*

There's an old frail man living under a bridge. His bed is in a large cardboard box. Everything he owns is in a shopping cart. His only friend is his loyal dog. His eyes expressively tell a story of loss and pain as a tear runs down his wrinkled cheek. At one time he had it all. He was living the American dream. His nightmare began the day a drunk driver took the lives of his wife and child. He would never be the same. *Have you ever passed by this man?*

Another woman; this one is just a teenager, age 18. She's all alone, estranged from her family, and almost 7 months pregnant. She lost her waitressing job because she could no longer fit in the uniform. Having nowhere to go and knowing that she must have a place to bring her baby home, she made the decision to save her money and be homeless for the remainder of her pregnancy. It's the middle of the winter on Christmas Eve; she finds shelter in an outdoor Nativity Scene on the property of a local church. She's sobbing but somehow feels comforted resting among the statues of The Holy Family. *I know this woman; she is my mother. (Factual, not fabricated)*

**Conclusion:** "For I was hungry and you gave me food, I was thirsty and you gave me drink, I was a stranger and you welcomed me, I was naked and you clothed me." "Truly, I say to you, as you did it to one of the least of my brothers, you did it to me." ~Matthew 25:35-45 (ESV)~

# Female Predator

Here's a poem for the ladies.
    Most can relate.
When another woman
    makes a move on your mate.

She's overly friendly
    each time they meet.
Her flirtatious actions
    are far from discreet.

She knows he's married,
    and happily, too.
Does she not see
    he'll always be true?

You don't lose your temper.
    You don't make a scene.
Her reputations at risk.
    Yours remains clean.

I feel sorry for women

   who act this way.

Grasping for attention

   with the games they play.


If you have a good man

   She'll never be a competitor.

Keep your happiness intact.

   She's just a **Female Predator**.

# Female Predator Inspiration

*Ok ladies, most of us know what it's like to be on either side of this scenario; so, let's be honest shall we?*

When you were single you have to admit there were times when you were envious of another woman who seemed to have *"the perfect guy."* You'd even find yourself intentionally attempting to get his attention in the hopes that their relationship might not be strong. It's ok to admit it. After all, you can't take a man away. *He walks away.* If he leaves easily, the relationship truly didn't stand a chance. I certainly don't condone flirting with engaged or married men; however, unfortunately I've known women who had no boundaries with an *"all's fair in love and war"* attitude. *I was not one of those women,* but *I was of the opinion* that a couple whose only dating is entirely different. That would also depend on how serious they were. This is easy to determine. *How?* It's been my experience that if a man is willing to flirt back then he's not into the one he's with. If he's worth holding on to then it's up to the woman to make certain that he knows *"she's the woman of his dreams."* If he doesn't realize that or treats her as such, then she's NOT and obviously he's NOT worth holding on to.

Moving into the future, you're now with a man who is *"your perfect guy."* You are finally on the *side* you wanted. You're blissfully happy and it shows. You know what that means right? Here they come, the women who used to be you. *"Wink."*

**Conclusion:** If you're just dating, remember the mind-set of the single woman looking for what you have. She's watching for an opportunity. If you're engaged or happily married, she may be deterred. However, like I mentioned above I've known woman who were quite aggressive in their endeavors. NO shame.

Either way, if you have a good man and a strong, loving relationship nothing or no one will come between you. Most people, including singles truly do enjoy a good love story and a happy ending even if it's not their own.

# Friendship, Betrayal, Recovery

What should you do
   when you feel betrayed
by a close friend
   who has temporarily strayed?

My advice to you
   is discuss the offense,
don't let it fester
   and cause more pretense.

They may be innocent,
   unaware of the pain.
Give them a chance,
   an opportunity to explain.

If they are guilty
   but filled with remorse;
listen, but make clear
   their behavior isn't endorsed.

If the explanation's satisfactory

    and the apology sincere,

put it behind you;

    don't shed another tear.


Weigh pros and cons

    after a painful discovery

to determine the worth

    of your friendships recovery.

# Friendship, Betrayal, Recovery Inspiration

*When it comes to my closest circle of friends, I'm selective. I'm talking about the friends that I would drop everything for. I've got their back even if I don't agree with them. I share my secrets and know they're safe. There's trust. There's a bond. These are the friends that I could go months without speaking with or even years without seeing; but we always pick up where we left off. They're family. It's unconditional. It's understood. I feel truly blessed to have them in my life.*

*You know the friends I'm speaking of, right? Unfortunately, it's these friends that can hurt you the most because you love them. You're not guarded with them. You're free to be your true self, which makes you vulnerable. They know things that your husband, wife, partner, or relatives may not know about you. So, if they hurt you, even unintentionally it's more painful.*

Back in the day my favorite group of party girls had a *"sister code"*. We would affectionately call each other *"my girls"* or *"mine."* We would never date an ex or a guy one of us was interested in without checking first. We each had a couple of *"favs"* that we all knew were *"untouchable"* by any of us except for the friend who made it clear, *"hands off."* It didn't matter whether there were real feelings for a particular guy or if they were just a good time guy. *It was understood.* It prevented awkwardness, hurt feelings, and kept our friendships strong. Guys came and went but we were always there for each other, and we still are to this day. It was a great code; until the day it was almost broken, on me.

I was anticipating a Saturday morning call from one of *"mine"* (I'll call her Alley) to tell me all about the Friday night fun I missed at a local hotspot.

To my dismay the conversation was not at all what I expected. She told me she had seen one of my *"favs"* (I'll call him Jason) and he asked her out. I was somewhat surprised because Jason had been on my *"favs fun list"* for several years. Never believing she would accept his invite, the only response I could come up with was; *"Wow, how did you handle that?"* Her answer was cavalier; *"I'm thinking about it."* Those four words in that particular tone stirred up a myriad of emotions. *Did I hear that right? She was informing me! Was one of "mine" actually going to break the code after all these years?* At first, I was in disbelief. We were tight. We both had numerous opportunities to break the code over the years; all of us had but never did. I felt betrayed, hurt, and angry. Once it sunk in, I was revved up and ready to set her straight! Promptly, I reminded her of the code. My anger then triggered some unpleasant, factual threats. I affirmed that I would continue seeing him (out of spite), her *"favs"* would now become mine as well, and our friendship would be over. We either put this behind us or *it's on!* I assured her that in spite of a temporary lapse in her judgment, our friendship would recover depending on her decision. *She made the right choice and we're still close friends to this day.*

**Conclusion:** You may think this sophomoric and my reaction harsh, I don't. We were all in agreement of the *"sister code"*, a code of **trust** and **loyalty** that was in place for years. Both are important character traits that I don't take lightly when broken. Ok, yes, he was contemptible to ask out my friend but boys in the *"fun category"* will most definitely be boys, and boys will come and go. However, friends as close as all of us, will be friends forever. I never spent time with him after that. It was too damaging for him to cross that line between friends. Oddly enough as fun as he was, I never missed him.

# Two Faces

She smiles at you
   when you first meet.
She's warm and welcoming,
   and appears rather sweet.

She's nestled nicely
   within her circle of friends.
The matriarch of them all
   is the message she sends.

Be leery of this queen
   as she invites you in.
The warning signs are clear.
   She's not a true friend.

You're safe when you face her,
   as she forms her close pack.
It's when you turn around
   that the knife strikes your back.

We've all met this person.

 We all can relate.

Her self-proclaimed power,

 does not discriminate.


Be alert to the clues,

 in large or small traces.

Beware of the smile

 that has **Two Faces**.

# Two Faces Inspiration

*We all have encountered this person at one time or another in our lives. As for myself; yes, the inspiration here is about a particular woman, but in the same sense; it describes several that I know, that likely we all know. I will, however; share the story behind the woman who inspired this poem. I'll call her Pat.*

Pat was born and raised in a small town. She appeared to be well-liked, kind, generous, and thoughtful. At first, I was sucked in by her charm, but it didn't take long for her true colors to seep through the exterior of her façade. At first it was subtle. I would be out with Pat and her friend; I'll call her Martha; to see them together one would think they were the best of friends. Once Martha would leave, Pat would tell me unflattering stories about her. At first, I was surprised at the stories themselves, but that soon changed to questions of why she would tell me this about her "close" friend? Getting to know Pat, I realized that this was the norm for her. It wasn't always about a particular friend; it was about any friend whenever the opportunity presented itself. It soon dawned on me; I wasn't immune to her deceitfulness and grateful I never shared anything personal with her. I was fond of several people I met through Pat and began resenting her for being so incredibly *two-faced* to them because they seemed to genuinely like her. How did they not see what I saw? Did they, and did they choose the illusion over the reality? Not wanting to alienate myself from those I truly liked in this circle of friends, I decided not to indulge in attempting to bring out her truth. Rather, I slowly distanced myself from her and stayed connected with those I enjoyed and respected.

Should I have shared what I knew? No. Others were present with her as well when she trashed characters and broke confidences. I was; however, the newcomer. I chose to rise above the fray and take myself out of an undesirable situation.

It's been years since I've been in her company. Since I've withdrawn from her circle of deceit, I have had the privilege of speaking with people who know her as I do. I find comfort in knowing that all those who come in contact with her aren't deceived.

**Conclusion:** Just because you're born and raised in a small town doesn't mean you're entitled to respect and the benefits of a close community. Small town people are loyal and protective of their own. You need to earn respect and prove that you're worthy of acceptance and friendships.

# Hidden Truth

Yes, I have your number.
    I see the real you.
You hide behind a façade.
    Your falseness I see through.

You're kind to my face
    when others are in view.
Snide remarks behind the scenes,
    when it's just us two.

You tell secrets of others
    that should never be told.
If your betrayal was known
    the hurt would surely unfold.

When I confronted your behavior,
    you showed concern and surprise.
Spewing lies to suit you,
    knowing I unmasked your disguise.

Your attitude has changed direction,
    sharing your story of woe.
I felt sorry for you,
    but still enjoyed the show.

I left you feeling confident
    I was on your side.
This is my false façade.
    My conscience is my guide.

For the sake of others
    I'll keep your **hidden truth**.
But I am watching you.
    Quietly, I am a sleuth.

IM WATCHING YOU

# Hidden Truth Inspiration

*How could I tell my dear friend (I'll call him Doug) that his new wife (I'll call her Pamela) is untrustworthy and careless with his privacy? I couldn't. I didn't. Could you, would you? Read on and decide for yourself.*

Out of the blue I get a call from Doug. I thought this was one of our catch-up calls because it had been months since we last spoke. He blurts out in excitement, "I'm married!" My shocked response was, "What? When? I mean, we just spoke six months ago and you were single with no interests." He began to tell me the story of how they were in love during their senior year of high school and reconnected at their school's thirty-fifth class reunion. He admitted their romance rekindled quickly, but when life gives you a second chance at love you don't let it slip away. He ended with a hopeful statement, "Please be happy for me Steph." *Wow! Well alright then.* There was no way I was going to burst his bubble of happiness. He had been lonely for years. I congratulated him and told him she must be pretty special to have won his heart, a second time.

He then proceeds to put her on the phone which began an uncomfortable conversation, for me. Let's just say in about fifteen minutes, *seriously*, fifteen minutes is all it took; she shared *waaaay* too much intimate and personal information about Doug *that can't be unheard*. I was in shock! Doug, who's very protective of his privacy, would be crushed and mortified by this betrayal. *I felt mortified for him!* I kept trying to change the subject until finally I cut her off telling her that she had no right to tell me any of this, and Doug might even think it unforgiveable if he knew.

For the first time in fifteen minutes, she was quiet. However, I continued to speak. I asked her what would compel her to share such information, especially with one of his closest friends that she's known for "five minutes (on the phone)?" *Well actually, fifteen minutes.* She answered tearfully that she was attempting to bond with me by sharing confidences like girlfriends do. She continued to cry, pleading with me not to tell Doug. She loved him, she was sorry, and he was everything to her. She then felt the need to tell me she had been in an abusive relationship about a year ago, and being with Doug changed her whole life for the better. I have to admit her story did pull at my heart strings.

My initial thought was he needs to get as far away from her as possible. Her lack of boundaries and pathetic logic for sharing Doug's secrets with me were concerning; then I remembered how excited he was telling me about her, and his ever-so-evident happiness. I told her the Doug I know and love is a kind, sensitive soul who's easily wounded because he's so trusting.

I agreed not to tell him of her offense because they're already married, and right now she's making him happy. However, I warned her if that changes, I will safeguard him from further pain. She had no choice but to except what I said, like it or not. Unfortunately, my blunt forwardness caused her to resent me, leading to underhanded insults and subtle snide remarks at every opportunity, all occurring in Doug's absence of course. I chose to be amused by her, which only added to her annoyance. Doug was happy and that's what truly mattered to me.

**Conclusion:** Sometimes *ya' just gotta suck it up* for the better good. Doug was happily clueless and as long as she kept *his* secrets, I would keep *hers*. Pretty fair agreement, I think.

# Education

A good education
    is an important tool;
but your success isn't measured
    by the years you attend school.

Education can come
    from many different sources.
Not only the classroom;
    but parents, life, and higher forces.

Your character and values;
    how you live your life are what count.
Not the ladder you climb
    or highest plateau that you mount.

Never devalue yourself
    or your self-worth underestimate.
Your life is important
    no matter how simple or ornate.

Life's lessons learned
   are quite essential;
in establishing who you are
   and reaching your full potential.


If you don't have a degree,
   don't feel inferior.
Be happy with the person
   looking back in the mirror.

# Education Inspiration

*Are you someone who never went to college and sometimes feel inadequate because of it? Maybe you didn't go because your life's circumstance didn't allow it. Maybe you thought you'd go someday, but some day still hasn't come. Maybe you're like me; taking courses here and there but never truly interested in making the commitment. No matter your reason, it's important to realize that the lack of a college education doesn't define who you are as a person. Read on.*

I was attending a large social event and sitting at a table surrounded by scholars who were all sharing stories about their alma mater. The conversation turned towards me and I was asked the inevitable question, "So where did you matriculate?" When I told them I never graduated from college, the next question was; "Well, what is it that you do?" When I told them I retired when I got married, there were no more questions for me. In a condescending tone, the final statement was, "Oh, that's nice too." I was no longer part of the conversation that evening. I wasn't given an opportunity to talk about what I did before I was married or share any of my interests. *There was no interest in me.* Suddenly I felt uncomfortable and inferior. I was saddened to think I wasn't worthy of them. Inferiority is a vulnerable feeling.

I thought about what happened for days. I even lost sleep lamenting over it. Why was I allowing this to affect my life? A hand full of people who I don't know didn't accept me. *So what*! Unlike them I am a person with character. I began to think about all the blessings in my life which includes some pretty amazing (and well educated) people who love me for me. I have compassion and respect for others.

I'm happy with the person looking back at me in the mirror. I quote my husband when I say, "There is no correlation between being well-educated and having good character."

**Conclusion:** No one can make you feel inferior without your consent. ~ Eleanor Roosevelt~

# The Nest

You've been given the tools.
　　You've learned right from wrong.
It's time to leave the nest.
　　Be brave and be strong.

You'll make some poor decisions.
　　Try not to be concerned.
It's part of life's journey.
　　Your experiences are lessons learned.

When you find yourself struggling,
　　remember you never are alone.
I'm always here for you.
　　Just pick up the phone.

Be excited and be happy.
　　You're now ready to embark.
The world is anxiously waiting.
　　Go and make your mark.

It is your turn now,
　　to make your own way.
I'm so proud of you,
　　more than words can say.

Letting go of my baby
　　is not a small feat.
Combating tears happy and sad,
　　is overwhelming and so bittersweet.

Everything I've done in life,
    you'll always be the best.
Take my love with you
    as you leave **The nest**.

# The Nest Inspiration

*What comes to your mind when you hear the words "The Nest?" I took a small poll and found most people said a bird's nest, others smiled and thought of a woman nesting during pregnancy, and some even said nesting boxes, etc., while very few thought of someone leaving "The Nest". I found that to be interesting since it was the first thought for me. Here's how "The Nest" came to be.*

I was reading through the social media on Face Book and noticed that many of my high school friends were posting how they were feeling about their children heading off to college. My first thought was, *"Wow, my high school friends have college age kids! When did that happen?"*

As I continued to read on, I noticed they had similar feelings about their children leaving home; a combination of pride and happiness due to successful parenting which prepared their children for independence, but there was a slight overshadowing of this wonderful accomplishment; bittersweet heartache.

Although I don't have children, I can relate to them in how my mom felt the day I left to get married and moved three thousand miles away from home. We've always been close, especially with me being an only child. We lived in the same town for 42 years spending quite a bit of quality time together. She felt like she was losing her daughter as well as her best friend. We were both beyond happy that I was marrying the man of "our" dreams and beginning another chapter of my life, but at the same time we both felt a sense of loss; bittersweet heartache.

**Conclusion:** Sometimes change isn't always as easy as it is necessary, especially when you feel like you're the one being left behind. It can be difficult to be comforted by the happiness of the one who's leaving when you're feeling a loss. I know this will sound a bit cliché, however; truly loving someone is letting them go if that's what they need and want. If you're the one who is leaving the nest to follow your dreams, make your way in the world, or just need a change in your life; be conscientious of those who love you and have to let you go. They will miss you.

## Opinion

They ask for your opinion
   after they've shared their news.
It's important to think
   about the words you choose.

Your thoughts hold value
   at the moment they ask.
As simple as this appears,
   It's a troublesome task.

Are they looking for the truth?
   Or what they really want to hear?
It's difficult to know.
   The answer is unclear.

Err on the side of caution
   if you haven't got a clue.
An incorrect response
   could change their opinion of you.

Do your thoughts in this matter
   truly hold any dominion?
If unsure, be wise
   and to yourself keep your **Opinion**.

# Opinion Inspiration

This poem speaks for itself. It's inspired by all of you who are chuckling or nodding right now just thinking about the last time someone asked for your opinion. Maybe you had a good outcome, maybe not. Either way, no one is immune from being asked the question, *"What do you think?"* One wouldn't think that a short question formed of four simple words would be cause for concern, right? Wrong, especially when it follows frustrated venting or an emotional tantrum. It could be a friend who just ended a long-term relationship, a colleague venting about their boss or co-worker, a family member upset with a sibling, or even gossip among acquaintances. Regardless, the person or people who are doing the asking are usually looking for quick validation. Unless you are confident with your opinion or the relationship between you and the person asking, *don't do it.* Somehow those much-needed words of affirmation that were so appreciated at the time, are suddenly twisted and used against you. Has this happened to you? *Sure it has.* Let me guess; you're thinking of a particular instance as you're reading this and wishing you had *kept your opinion to yourself.*

**Conclusion:** Be a good listener. Unspoken words can't be used against you.

# Wear Your Masks/Covid-19

**YOU:**  Wearing a mask is uncomfortable.
It makes me feel claustrophobic.
**ME:**    Yes, it can feel confining.
The alternative is getting sick.

**YOU:**  They fog up my glasses,
making it difficult to see.
**ME:**    Yes, it's a small inconvenience
for all of our safety.

**YOU:**  It's safe to gather unmasked
with friends, people I know.
**ME:**    But where have they been?
Maybe their symptoms don't show.

**YOU:**  My freedom is being suppressed.
Wearing a mask is unnecessary.
**ME:**    The death tolls are rising.
Don't you find that scary?

**YOU:**  The news is outta control.
It **IS** an election year.
**ME:**    Are you truly that ignorant,
believing they're falsely instilling fear?

**YOU:**  I don't like wearing masks,
they make breathing too challenging.
**ME:**    Would being on a ventilator
be less difficult or ravaging?

**YOU:**  You're taking this too seriously.
　　　　It's similar to the flu.
**ME:**　Your attitude is quite cavalier.
　　　　I feel concern for you.

　　　The truth of the matter…
　　　　　is everyday people are dying.
　　　We're all in this together.
　　　　　So why aren't you trying?


　　　This virus is dangerously formidable.
　　　　　Experts have given easy tasks.
　　　Stop being careless and selfish.
　　　　　Be proactive, **wear your masks**.

# Wear Your Masks/COVID-19 Inspiration

*It's the year 2020 and unless you're living under a rock, you're aware of the deadly Coronavirus (COVID-19) that is attacking the world and changing our way of life. This formidable evil force has taken more lives in the last eight months than the Revolutionary War, Korean War, Vietnam War, 911, and the War on Terror combined. Every day this number increases in The United States and Globally. If you contract this virus and you're fortunate enough to survive, you'll likely have long-term serious health ramifications such as respiratory and cardiac issues. This is not to be taken with a dismissive attitude. THIS IS A FACT!! Specialists and experts repeatedly tell us how we can slow the spread and stay safe while a vaccine is being produced and tested; wear a mask, social distance, and wash your hands frequently. Don'tcha' think these are simple rules to follow? Well apparently, not for some.*

I wrote this poem feeling frustrated after numerous conversations with people who refuse to wear a mask. Some of their reasons were understandable and even relatable, *but not acceptable.* It makes no sense to me that if you have the ability to take the necessary precautions to protect yourself and others, especially those who are vulnerable and already unhealthy; *why you wouldn't.* It should be a "no-brainer."

**Conclusion:** If you're someone who chooses not to wear a mask, please reconsider. You have the power to make a difference. To help save lives and protect each other is a required responsibility of us all. *We're in this together.* We need to participate in the battle against this fierce virus that is taking so much from us; everything from the necessities of life and keeping us separated from loved ones to causing serious illness and death.

Let's beat this together by being *in this together*, be proactive. What an *awe*-inspiring act it is to be doing something that contributes to the well-being of everyone. Go for it! Put your mask on. Be *awe*some!

For those of you who are on the "front lines" in the hospitals, checking on your neighbors and elderly, running errands for those who are at a high risk, for all the businesses offering curb side and home delivery, for everyone who's taking the recommended steps to keep us all protected showing this virus the respect it deserves, **THANK YOU** for being *AWE*some!

# Revenge

Whether you're all alone
    or out in full view;
when you're seeking revenge
    you can't hide from you.

Think twice before you
    intentionally hurt another.
listen to that built-in emotion
    that affects you like no other.

It's a feeling you get
    from deep down within.
A moment of conscience,
    when you're about to sin.

Your actions and words
    can seal your fate.
They'll follow you through life
    from the mess you create.

Let it go. Move on.
    It's not an act of defeat.
Rise above the fray.
    **Revenge** is not always sweet.

# Revenge Inspiration

*Revenge; a feeling we've all felt at one time or another in our lives. It can best be described as an overwhelming need for retaliation on those who've hurt you. Sometimes it can be achieved quickly with an immediate "tit for tat" sort of retort if you were hurt by another's rudeness or remarks. Revenge in this case is usually short and sweet. It's the personal satisfaction of getting even and isn't that what revenge is all about? There are many types of revenge ranging from poetic justice to revenge tragedy. Revenge can be difficult to suppress when your wound is new. Some people can be blinded by their need for revenge. They're consumed by thoughts of how to harm those who've caused them emotional or physical suffering. This is unhealthy. It can turn into a dangerous cycle that can lead to the loss of life-long friendships, lives can be ruined, and in severe cases lives can be lost.*

We're all human. We're not immune to our emotions. It's our nature to defend ourselves, *but at what cost?* This poem is meant to be tool to cause you to pause and think before acting out. Try to think about cause and effect in a selfless nature. Instead of reacting in the same poor behavior; rise above it. Why? Well let me ask you a question. How many times in your life have you said or done something that hurt someone, and then felt regret? Perhaps you are thinking of that moment right now and feeling that if you could go back in time and change it, you would. Admit it. We all do. It's quite possible the person who hurt you is feeling that way. So why not stop the vicious cycle of revenge. Isn't it more empowering to take control of your own actions in a positive manner than to consciously hurt another? It's likely that if someone is consistently and constantly harmful to others, they'll cause their own destruction.

**Conclusion:** What a nicer world we'd live in if we used our God given freedom to make choices by choosing forgiveness.

If you're still not convinced and want to seek revenge, how about this one: The best revenge is to be unlike him who performed the injury. ~Marcus Aurelius~

# Holding a Grudge

When someone hurts or offends you,
   it's easy to hold a grudge.
We are all human that way,
   to be stubborn; unwilling to budge.

Sometimes we can be too sensitive,
   taking others actions or words personally.
It's easier to hold a grudge
   rather than forgive or act mercifully.

Maybe you're in the wrong place
   after they've had a bad day.
It's difficult to let it slide
   and to rise above the fray.

It could be that they're struggling
   or physically hurting in some way.
Their emotional health is in trouble.
   Something's keeping their happiness at bay.

Here's a challenge for us all.
   I'm giving you a gentle nudge.
Let it go, pray for them.
   Find peace not **Holding a Grudge**.

Forgiveness

# Holding a Grudge Inspiration

*No doubt you can think of people who've hurt or offended you in some way and you held it against them for the longest time; maybe you're still holding on to it. If you've let it go and moved on, awesome and good for you! If not, I'm sure you have your reasons but truth be told; life is way too short to hold a grudge.*

I write about forgiveness quite a bit in my poetry and inspirations because I truly believe it's important for your own physical and emotional well-being. Hatred and resentment can wreak havoc on your psyche; and ultimately cause much more damage to you than the original offense.

**Conclusion:** Forgiveness is powerful. Forgiveness is a choice, *your choice.* It's always possible to forgive, even if reconciliation is not. Forgiveness doesn't mean condoning. It's a way to let go of the offense that is keeping you in the *"victim"* role. Forgiveness is the first step to letting go of a grudge. Don't let a grudge define who you are or keep you from being the best you, and living your best life. Go ahead-give it try, you'll be so glad you did.

# Glory to God

*As the years pass, I sometimes look back on my life and think about the choices I made, some good, some great, and some not so much. I think about the people who came into my live and stayed, while others seemed to fade into the background or even disappeared from my memory; and the times when I met challenges successfully as well as the times I felt I failed terribly. Through all of life's highs, lows, and changes there is the presence of God, undeniably steadfast and true.*

*This next section I am sharing with you my relationship with God, love for God, and some of my personal experiences. If you believe in God, I have no doubt you'll find some relatable. If you are not a believer, I hope you'll feel inspired to open your heart to the possibilities and wonders of having a relationship with God during your journey through this life.*

# My Lord and Savior. My friend and Comforter.

# My Defender and Protector.

Whenever God answers a prayer, it supersedes my expectations. It's always better than my request. I just know God's hands are on it, because it's perfection.

Of course God, like any Father sometimes says no. This is the time for trusting that He knows what's best for me. Even on my worst days, I know he's with me sharing my pain. That's when I hold on to his promises, keep my faith, and know that I am in great hands. It's the safest place on earth to be.

# The Presence of You

You knew me first.
   That's what I read.
You're always with me.
   That's what you said.

When mom introduced us
   early in my life,
I felt a connection.
   Peace, absent of strife.

I made some mistakes.
   I'm human that way.
You'd always be waiting,
   even when I'd stray.

Always welcoming me back
   with arms opened wide.
Ready to forgive me;
   your love never denied.

Your love is unconditional,
   understanding as I pray.
Through highs and lows,
   you're here to stay.

As I look back,

my life in review;

there is no denying

**the presence of you**.

# The Presence of You Inspiration

*God has a way of communicating with you that may only be evident to you, in a way that only you understand. It's individualized and unique to you. It's not difficult to see, feel, or hear God's presence if you just pay attention and spend time with Him. He's with you.*

I'm in a car with four friends and the driver becomes careless on the wet, winding road of the Mohawk Trail. There were cliffs and sharp curves all along the way. He thinks it's funny that I'm crying and telling him to slow down. I laid myself down on the backseat and prayed to keep us safe. I prayed for a small accident, just enough to stop him but with no one getting hurt. Within moments we didn't make a corner, but instead of driving off a cliff, there was a side road that he was able to gear off on; putting us in a small ditch. It slowed him down and we got home safely. I never got back in a car with him again. *That was God answering my prayer. It was exact.*

I'm attending mass the weekend before I am to get results from a biopsy. I'm afraid of the potential results and I'm praying I'll be ok; when as clear as day I hear whispered in my ear *"You're going to be ok."* I was. The results were negative.

I participate in weekly Adoration. For those of you who don't know what Adoration is, its dedicated time spent with God in front of the Monstrance, (which holds the consecrated host) in God's presence. I was going through some personal struggles and I was looking directly at the consecrated host during my prayers when I saw the image of Christ's face. I could clearly see the outline of His eyes, nose, mouth, and hair.

I was in awe and sobbed uncontrollably. I felt overwhelmed with love and comfort. *It was an immensely profound experience.* That same image has presented itself to me multiple times since then, during my time in the Adoration Chapel.

I could be thinking about something, anything *specific* and within hours or days it appears or happens. I believe that is God's way of letting me know He's listening to me whether I'm talking to him out loud or in my thoughts, He hears me.

**Conclusion:** I have many stories of God's presence and love surrounding me, protecting me, and bringing the right people into my life in my time of need. Whether it's obviously evident or subtle, *I feel Him. I trust Him.*

# Pause

Whenever you are having doubts,
    pause and look all around.
God's presence is evidently everywhere
    through sight, touch, and sound.

The infinity of the sky
    as the clouds form shapes.
A slide show from Heaven
    showing us a wondrous skyscape.

You feel God's gentle caress
    from a warm summer breeze;
leaving a sense of calm,
    putting your mind at ease.

Now close your eyes slightly
    and listen to the sounds,
of the birds singing songs;
    your soul, God's peace surrounds.

These are a few gifts
    that God gave us free.
Don't take them for granted.
    **Pause**; listen, feel, and see.

# Pause Inspiration

*Life is busy with endless challenges to face almost daily. The news seems to always spout the negative that is going on in the world, repeatedly and endlessly. Let me ask you, how often do you take the time to "pause" and take in the beauty that God has placed in your life?*

It's early in the morning and I just happen to look outside at the right moment to see a doe drinking from the birdbath. I walk outside and she just looks at me unaffected by my presence. She doesn't run. She's beautiful! I'm ready to go inside when here comes her fawn. No fear. No threat. *I feel doubly blessed.*

I look at the sky and see the formation of a rabbit, then a duck, and then finally I see a ray of sun peeking through. It's peaceful. It's lovely. *It's God's artistry.*

I'm working in the yard when out of nowhere a butterfly lands on my hand. I raise it up to my face to get a better look. We looked at each other. It never flew away until I encouraged it to. A similar thing happened with a dragonfly. I actually was petting its wings and again, it didn't move until I encouraged it. *What a beautiful, rare occurrence.*

It's a hot, humid summer day with no breeze; the kind of day that you seem to wear the air and sweat instantly. I'm outside watering flowers and feeling quite miserable when a comforting breeze gives me relief. I call moments like this a *Kiss from God.*

How about the songs of birds? Have you ever truly listened to the *beautiful, musical sounds* they make, and how soothing it can be? They always *make me smile.*

How lovely. All this nature is free. I like to call these *"gifts from God"* a little taste of Heaven.

**Conclusion:** When others may see only natural occurrences and "coincidences," I see miracles and *signs of God* at work in my life. Even if your perspective isn't the same as mine, take time to enjoy the *"pause"* moments of your life.

# Believe

He doesn't ask for much
    for the path He paved.
It's such a small request
    from the lives He saved.

Making it easy for us
    to follow ten simple commands.
He even gave us prayers
    that echo across the lands.

He never breaks his promises.
    Heavens eternity we will receive.
Blessings, graces, and everlasting life
    for those who truly **Believe.**

# Believe Inspiration

*I believe that everything that happens during your life's journey is God's way of preparing you for eternity. I like to call myself "a work in progress." I'm unfinished. True, we're all perfection in God's eyes; but free-will can change our destination. **Meaning:** you can choose not to believe in God and everlasting life.*

I look at life as an opportunity to get it right. This is the time to make mistakes, but learn from them. To be the best "human-being" you can be. I don't mean by climbing the corporate ladder or making millions, although that's wonderful if that's your life's path and you use it wisely by helping others who are less fortunate. Whatever your path in life is; don't live it like you're alone in this world by being selfish and self-serving. Any advantages in life that you have are blessings from God, *gifts*. I'm just stating it's best to share your gift(s) with others who could benefit from it. Then, you become a gift from God to them. *Can you see the potential in the different acts of kindness and generosity that creates a beautiful circle of love in life?* Doesn't it make sense, *common sense?* You would think living your life as a race and not as an individual could and would make all the difference in the world.

**Conclusion:** "You shall love the Lord your God with all your heart, with all your soul, and with all your mind. And the second is like it: You shall love your neighbor as yourself."

~Matthew 22:37-39

God gave us the tools we need and the free will to use them wisely. We have prayers, books, The Ten Commandments, and countless/endless opportunities to know Him. God showers us with his grace all the time and shows us his presence everywhere. You just have to be receptive. *Open your heart.* He's there, waiting. Life without God is unimaginable to me.

**I Believe.**

# The Man of My Dreams

**(My husband, Robert J. Jackson)**
**(a.k.a. Handsome)**

With You, Life Is Beautiful

# Robert J. Jackson (The Man of My Dreams)

*My husband (I'll refer to as Handsome) truly is in my opinion,* **the crème de la crème** *when it comes to men.*

## Our love story of how we met:

You could say we were first introduced by his parents, Eddie and Rita, about six years before we actually met. *Confused?* Let me elaborate. Eddie and Rita were originally from my home town. They would come for long visits (from Texas) to spend time with family and friends. In 1996 they decided to stay with their niece (E.T.) who happened to be my mom's roommate. I instantly liked them. They were an interesting and fun couple. Apparently, I must've made a good impression on them as well because they started to tell me about their son who was single, close to my age, in the Navy, and would undoubtedly like me. I told them I had a few pen-pals who were in the service and enjoyed reading about their travels, especially being a small-town girl who, with the exception of Canada, had never been beyond the upper east coast states. They encouraged me to write to him. *I am so glad I did.*

Like I stated above, our written communication lasted six years. During that period of time, I not only got to know *Handsome* better, but his parents as well. In 1998 I went to Texas to spend time with them when Rita was having some health issues and wanted me to come see her home. It was the first time I had ever flown. Fortunately, I didn't fly alone. Mom and E.T. went as well. Little did I know then, it wouldn't be long before I was flying across the country on a regular basis to spend time with their son. (*God surely had plans for us.*)

In 1998 Mom, E.T., and I decided to rent a house together. It was a large 17-room house; I occupied a four-room suite upstairs. It was nice for us to be all together after me living alone for nearly 10 years, but with each of us still having our own private space. I mention this because in December of 2002 Eddie and Rita came to stay with us for the Christmas holiday. *Handsome* decided to take leave and come from overseas to stay as well. It was wonderful that we had plenty of room to accommodate everyone. I remember having mixed emotions of excitement and nervousness to be finally meeting him face to face. When we were writing, I knew there was something special about him. I felt a connection that I knew he felt too, because of the change in his correspondences from platonic to flirtatious.

Everyone arrived at different times, but on the same night. It was December 18th. E.T. and I picked *Handsome* up at the airport. He kissed me hello on the cheek and I felt butterflies in my stomach. I kept wondering, *"What is it about him?"* I was like a school girl with a crush.

For the next couple of days, we *"all"* had a great time together. But now it was time for *"us."* I had made plans for the two of us to see Miss Saigon at Proctors in New York for Saturday evening, December 21st. That evening changed everything for me. It confirmed that he was different from other guys, and I wanted to know more about him.

The following January 2003, I moved into an apartment because the house we all lived in was being sold that spring. Although it was sad to leave after being roomies with E.T. and mom for five years, it worked out for the best giving *Handsome* and I *"complete privacy"* when he'd come to visit. *Ya' know what it's like when romance is in the air, right?*

Over the next two and half years he swept me off my feet. Even though it was a long-distance relationship, we made it work. We spoke almost every day when possible, wrote endless romantic letters, supported the airlines, and fell in love.

It was time to close the distance between us. He proposed January 3rd, 2005 and we were married September 2nd the same year.

Our love story continues......*stronger than ever!*

**Conclusion:** I can honestly say, although I had been in a couple of long-term relationships in my past where I said, "I Love You," I never *truly* knew what love was and what it *truly* meant until *Handsome*. There is NO comparison. I don't regret my past relationships because they made me realize what *I did* and *didn't* want in my life. Each person comes into your life for a reason. Each experience helps form the person you become. *Handsome* made me feel worthy of love like his. I can see myself looking across the table from him when we're old and frail knowing I made the right choice, feeling *joy* that *I got* to spend my life with such an incredible human-being, and thinking; how'd I get so lucky and what did I do in life to deserve such a gift, such a blessing?

As you turn the pages of the next three poems inspired by the man I married, you'll have more understanding of why he's also **The Man of My Dreams**.

# A Dream Come True

An interesting couple came to visit.
    They spoke of their military son.
Encouraging me to be his Pen-Pal,
    soon our written connection had begun.

We sent postcards, letters, and emails
    for a duration lasting six years.
He shared his stories of travel.
    I shared my dreams and fears.

The anticipation was just about over.
    We were finally going to meet.
Our written connection changed its direction,
    becoming more personal, flirtatious, and sweet.

I'll never forget how I felt
    when I first saw his face.
He leaned in, kissing my cheek
    with a warm and gentle embrace.

There was definitely a strong connection.
    A powerful attraction I couldn't deny.
My head spinning as I wondered,
    "Could this possibly be *The Guy*?"

We went on our first date
    to see the musical Miss Saigon,
followed by dinner and enjoyable conversation;
    getting familiar, we continued to bond.

That first date changed my life.
    I would never be the same.
Falling in love with him easily,
    I agreed to take his name.

My life wrapped in his love,
    made all my dreams a reality.
Filled with unconditional love and happiness,
    just the way life should be.


Each day I feel truly blessed,
    for men like him are few.
Once he was only a dream.
    Now he's **A Dream Come True**.

*September 2nd, 2005*

*Santa Fe, NM*

# My One True Love

Your actions have shown me
  that your feelings are true,
even long before you expressed
  the words *"I love you."*

You are loving and thoughtful,
  and your kindness never falters.
You are a sensitive man,
  and your temperament never alters.

You are always the gentlemen.
  You are faithful and honest.
You are handsome and intelligent,
  and you always remain modest.

Putting me on a pedestal,
  you've never let me fall;
always making me feel safe,
  putting my happiness above all.

Knowing my secrets are secure,
  tucked in your memories vault.
You are patient and forgiving
  when mistakes are my fault.

There is nothing I need.
  You give with full generosity.
Am I living a dream?
  No, it's my blessed reality.

I know in my heart
  You're a gift from above.
You're my first, my last,
    you're **My One True Love.**

# An Answered Prayer

Before there was you;
    there was a prayer,
for that special someone;
    my life to share.

I had certain specifics
    in my prayerful request.
God hand selected you,
    giving me his best.

I was often told
    there's no perfect guy.
Then I met you,
    making that a lie.

My life is complete.
    My life you share.
A gift from God,
    you're **An Answered Prayer.**

# In Loving Memory

**Mildred C. (Vanier) O'Grady**

**September 22, 1921 - August 20, 1997**

**(My Meme')**

Faith

Faith came singing into my room
        and other guests took flight.
Fear, anxiety, grief, and gloom
        sped out into the night.

I wondered how such peace could be
        but Faith said gently, don't you see?
Fear, anxiety, grief, and gloom
        really cannot live with me.

*Written by: Mildred C. Vanier-1937*

My Meme' wrote this beautiful poem when she was just 16 years old. What a lovely way to honor her memory by publishing her work in my book.

To me she was a passionate, caring, talented woman who enjoyed playing all types of games. We spent hour's playing cards and board games. She took care of me as a child while my mom worked. She was always there when I needed her. She was a wonderful listener and advice giver. She was truly a devoted grandmother whose love for me never faltered. We shared a bond. She was "My Meme'."

# Words Of Encouragement

I am really honored and touched that you shared your poetry with me. You are writing some beautiful, intensely personal, and profound prose that will deeply affect your readers. What I love most about your work is that the voice is so clearly *you*; your heart, your honesty, and your direct but gentle way of speaking your truth. This is absolutely your voice, which makes the reader know the poems are honest. I read them all earlier today, when I was at the library working, and then again at 5:00 when I returned home. They really resonate for me. I like the way your poetry is the culmination of a lot of soul-searching, personal understanding, and generosity of spirit. You've worked to arrive at the wisdom that shines through your poems. And to me, your poetry represents a form of closure for you. But not forgetting—they are your way of carrying forward your life experiences, which, of course, have shaped who you are. You've taken your life experiences and allowed them to make you a stronger, more thoughtful person. These are beautiful works—and beautifully expressed—that are very touching. Thank you so much for sharing them with me.

**~Stefanie J.**

What a beautiful poem! (Referring to "Homeless") It's very inspirational and enlightening, full of truth and kindness. You have a beautiful way of expressing a painful topic that our society can't seem to correct.

**~Patricia R.**

You are a very brave woman letting God use you as He is. You will never know the lives you will save when sensitive young women read your words. (Referring to "Unborn Apology")

**~Mary McConnell**

I am so very proud of you and admire the poetry you write. You inspire me every day to be a better person and I am certain that all who know you feel the same way.

**~Eileen O. (Mom)**

Read "The Presence of You" and am most appreciative of how you are allowing God to work through you to others through poetry. It's a gift.

**~Eunice T.**

I was so impressed with your writing; Steph and I hope you are keeping it up!

**~Carol D.**

Thank you for sharing your beautiful poems with me. You have a talent! You go girl! Keep those wonderful poems flowing. I would love to read more.

**~Julie D.**

Thank you so much
For reading my book!

If you would like to share your

thoughts with me, please

Email me at:

sjjacksonpoetry@yahoo.com

"Hope to hear from you!"

"

Made in the USA
Monee, IL
27 November 2021

83262819R00074